# Dragón Barbudo

# Bearded Dragon

# Lagartija Moteada Marrón

# Brown Spotted Gecko

# DISCOVER SERIES
# LIZARDS

# LAGARTIJAS

# Lagartija Monitor Argus

# Argus Monitor Lizard

# Lagartija Rayado Marrón

## Brown Striped Lizard

# Camaleón

# Chameleon

# Lagartija de Pincel

## Brush Lizard

# Cameleón Pantera

# Panther Chameleon

# Gecko Crestado

## Crested Gecko

# Broche Brillante de Lagartija

## Shiny Lizard Pin

# Lagartija de Cuello Volante

## Frill-Necked Lizard

# Gecko

# Gecko

# Monstruo Gila

# Gila Monster

# Iguana Verde

# Green Iguana

# Dragón de Agua Indio

# Indian Water Dragon

# Newt Warty de Laos

## Laos Warty Newt

# Gecko Leopardo

# Leopard Gecko

# Lagartija Monitor

# Monitor Lizard

# Camaleón Pantera

# Panther Chameleon

# Lagartija Monitor de Garganta Durazno

## Peach Throat Monitor Lizard

# Salamandra

# Salalmander

# Dragón Barbudo de Espalda de Seda sin Escamas

## Silkbacks Scaleless Bearded Dragon

# Gecko Tokay

# Tokay Gecko

# Camaleón Joven

# Young Chameleon

# Make Sure to Check Out the Other Discover Series Books from Xist Publishing:

Published in the United States by Xist Publishing
www.xistpublishing.com
PO Box 61593 Irvine, CA 92602

© 2018 by Xist Publishing All rights reserved
Translated by Victor Santana
No portion of this book may be reproduced without express permission of the publisher
All images licensed from Fotolia
First Bilingual Edition

ISBN: 978-1-5324-0671-3    eISBN: 978-1-5324-0672-0

Xist Publishing

www.ingramcontent.com/pod-product-compliance
Ingram Content Group UK Ltd.
Pitfield, Milton Keynes, MK11 3LW, UK
UKHW062045180426
11947UKWH00030B/2047